Aim for the Head
a collection of poetry

ɔ3

Derrick C. Brown & Rob Sturma, Editors

Write Bloody Publishing
America's Independent Press

Long Beach, CA

WRITEBLOODY.COM

D0002797

Brown, Derrick C.
Sturma, Rob.
1ˢᵗ edition.
ISBN: 978-1-935904-47-2

Interior Layout by Lea C. Deschenes
Cover Designed by Bill Jonas
Cover Art by David Ayllon
Interior Illustrations by Leigh White and Freedom Drudge
Proofread by Jennifer Roach
Edited by Derrick Brown and Rob Sturma
Re-loaded by Rob Sturma
Type set in Bergamo from www.theleagueofmoveabletype.com

Special thanks to Lightning Bolt Donor, Weston Renoud

Printed in Tennessee, USA

Write Bloody Publishing
Long Beach, CA
Support Independent Presses
writebloody.com

To contact the author, send an email to writebloody@gmail.com

Daphne Gottlieb's "fifteen ways to stay alive" appears courtesy of special permission by Manic D Press

John Paul Davis's "The Zombie, Rejected By His Human Lover, Responds" first published by Cordite Poetry Review

AIM FOR THE HEAD

AIM FOR THE HEAD

George Romero Never Lied to Us
by Ryk McIntyre

The dignity of zombie movies has always been the harsh face
we are shown of ourselves. The dead will always be the same:
equal parts hunger and will. They will always be conspicuous

consumption. We have changed. We don't fear the graveyard
as much as chemical spills. Don't listen for the Houngan drums,
it is the laboratory reports that are twined with magic programs,

reanimation cyphers; perfectly sterile, untouched by human hands
or even a single voice asking why. No wonder so many movies
begin in hospitals and research facilities. The sound of lab glass

breaking has devoured the *thud-thud-shhhh* of dirt being dug
from underneath. We have come so far in the future, we've flown
to the moon. But it's still the grave that claims our dreams, and feeds

us fear of being eaten alive. We could upload our individual death
on Youtube. It would be karmic justice on American terms: no worries
that God will call you home entirely. Pieces of us will walk forever.

TANKA: YET ANOTHER POEM ABOUT THE ZOMBIE APOCALYPSE PART 1

by Curtis X Meyer

That day—when at last
the zombie apocalypse
arrives —fuck the mall.
I'm going where I know it's
deserted: the library.

Fifteen Ways to Stay Alive
by Daphne Gottlieb

1. Offer the wolves your arm only from the elbow down. Leave tourniquet space. Do not offer them your calves. Do not offer them your side. Do not let them near your femoral artery, your jugular. Give them only your arm.

2. Wear chapstick when kissing the bomb.

3. Pretend you don't know English.

4. Pretend you never met her.

5. Offer the bomb to the wolves. Offer the wolves to the zombies.

6. Only insert a clean knife into your chest. Rusty ones will cause tetanus. Or infection.

7. Don't inhale.

8. Realize that this love was not your trainwreck, was not the truck that flattened you, was not your Waterloo, did not cause massive hemorrhaging from a rusty knife. That love is still to come.

9. Use a rusty knife to cut through most of the noose in a strategic place so that it breaks when your weight is on it.

10. Practice desperate pleas for attention, louder calls for help. Learn them in English, French, Spanish: May Day, Aidez-Moi, Ayúdeme.

11. Don't kiss trainwrecks. Don't kiss knives. Don't kiss.

12. Pretend you made up the zombies, and only superheroes exist.

13. Pretend there is no kryptonite.

14. Pretend there was no love so sweet that you would have died for it, pretend that it does not belong to someone else now, pretend like your heart depends on it because it does. Pretend there is no wreck—you watched the train go by and felt the air brush your face and that was it. Another train passing. You do not need trains. You can fly. You are a superhero. And there is no kryptonite.

15. Forget her name.

Gifts For the Dead at Christmas
by Andy Buell

blankets
worm repellent
a haircut
a manicure
a new suit to wear
pictures of who I grew into
letters to reintroduce myself

Apologies for not shedding tears when I heard the news. I promise
you it was only because I didn't understand, years later it was the
fermented spirits that held them back.

Tape recordings of my voice,
telling you how the bath felt
in the tub I still don't fit into,
I watched reflections of a savior
circle the drain for hours.

Reminders that you will never
have to deal with traffic again.

Finally waving goodbye
with my eyes open.

LEAVING ASHLEE
by John Andrews

in another life
your stomach hangs
with weight from our children
we are slow dancing
the kitchen is on fire
we don't turn
our heads
watch it burn
in this one
your stomach hangs
the weight of what could have been
I left you
on the front porch
shackled to a column
legs folded underneath
blood flowering out
your mouth
a hunger I could
never feed

Citizenship Test for the UUSA (United Undead States of America)
(data compiled by Rachelanne Williams)

Before continuing to the knowledge test, please fill out these identification questions. (We will not share any of your information with outside parties)

FULL NAME:* _____

> *If you cannot remember your full name due to the passage of time and deterioration of the brain, please make one up and carve it somewhere on your existing flesh so that you might remember it. Should you be accepted as a citizen, dog tags will be made for you.

SEX (circle one): Male Female Other*

> *Chose this option only if you have been dead too long to remember, and your private areas have rotted away, or if is possible you have missing ribs.

In what time period was your death?
A) Within the past 5 years
B) Between 5 and 10 years ago
C) Between 10 and 50 years ago
D) Between 50 and 100 years ago
E) More than 100 years ago*

*If you selected answer E please note the historical time period of your first life (Ex: French Revolution, Colonial America, Ancient Egyptian, Etc.) _____

Please choose the following that best describes you:
A) I have retained nearly all of my flesh (no visible bone structure)
B) My body consists of most of my original flesh (very little exposed bone)
C) My body consists of some flesh (rotted flesh clinging to bone)
D) I am a skeleton.

During the time of the plague, did you have a valid driver's license in one of the original 50 states? (y/n) If so, please copy down your license number. _____

Do you know how to use any post 1900 firearms? (y/n)

What is your marital status?
- A) I have never had a spouse
- B) My spouse is also a zombie
- C) My spouse died in the first wave of the plague
- D) I ate my spouse after becoming a zombie

If you have an(y) undead child(ren), please list their name(s) and age(s) in the following space:

Now your proctor will ask you to recite the Pledge of Undead Allegiance. If you cannot complete this, you will fail your test. For those without lower jaws or key facial/throat muscles, you may request this as a written portion.

KNOWLEDGE TEST

You will have 42 minutes to complete this portion of the test. This quiz tests your basic knowledge of Zombie History, Zombie Law, and Zombie Culture. Please note that failure of this test will result in the immediate cure of your living dead virus and prompt burial at sea. We apologize for the lasting effects of this death, but due to brain rationing, sacrifices must be made. Thank you for your cooperation.

When the proctor notes that it is time to begin, turn the page and begin your test.

The word *Zombie* comes from the…

A) Sound that is made as brains are sucked out of a human ear
B) Voodoo word for a curse cast by sorcerers causing mind control
C) Scientific term for the plague, zombificus silvocaniconiosis
D) Sound of an undead woman's sneeze

The most famous battle in the war against the living took place in Las Vegas, Nevada. What courageous undead leader directed the zombie armies to a stunning and heroic victory over the closed minded living humans?

A) General Eisenhower
B) Alexander the Great
C) Richard Nixon
D) Aslan the Lion
E) Oprah Winfrey

When entering a church, it is undead law to…
A) Remove your shoes
B) Drain blood into the bowl of holy water
C) Recite the first line of the Zombie Bible
D) Undead beings are not permitted inside Holy buildings.
E) None of the Above

How many times did our savior, Mr. Rogers, have to change his bloodstained sweaters in the battle for Houston, Texas?

A) 1-3
B) 3-5
C) 5 or more
D) Mr. Rogers was topless in the battle

True or False: In a court of zombie law, an undead person who has lost the flesh of one or both eyeballs can still testify as a witness, even when his/her decomposition might have deteriorated the plausibility of a valid statement.

True or False: Feeding another zombie salt (a poisonous substance) is punishable by life.

True or False: All zombies, even those that have decomposed to skeleton form, need at least 5 hours sleep every afternoon, even during the winter.

True or False: Decapitating a body infected with the plague will cause its immediate death, unless the head is left close enough to the body for it to be screwed back on by the corpse.

True or False: Zombie women may get pregnant and give birth to undead babies.

How many zombie states are there in the UUSA? _____

The national holiday celebrating zombie independence is on what date? _____

How many hours of sunlight can a zombie take before deteriorating beyond aid? _____

In what year did George A. Romero's *Night of the Living Dead* premiere? _____

Essay Portion:

Some say that the nature of a zombie apocalypse proves the notion that civilization is inherently fragile in the face of unprecedented diseases/ threats; they argue that most individuals cannot be relied upon to support the greater good if the personal cost becomes too high. How will you keep the UUSA a functioning civilization, rather than a mishmash of chaotic mummies foraging for brains selfishly? How would your unique skills help you to do this?

Please write your answer on a separate piece of paper.

REBIRTH IS ALWAYS PAINFUL
by Evan Peterson

after *Re-Animator*, directed in 1985 by Stuart Gordon

Today we play the meat card. The sticky.
Today innards uncoil like vines
and seize you by the ankle. The best elixirs
glow *[teenage lightning]*. We bless the syringe
and push into epidural space.
[Flush of bioluminescence: hormone geyser:
phosphorescence] Howling like a newborn,
dragged back from the cold and liquid
Afterworld for another go at breath,
a second death. Today we press some flesh.
Today we peel up the toenail. Ancient question:
when dead folks walk, do they know poetry?
Or is it all just hunger, brains, and meat?
Don't fool yourself; a zombie does feel pain.
It's the pain itself that has no meaning.

ZOMBIE STAND-UP
by Shappy Seasholtz

Thank you! Thank you!
What a wonderful audience!

There am nothing more beautiful than
the sound of rotting flesh slapping together!

That's what she said!

Me kidding, me kidding!
Me eat own penis long time ago—

Cuz that's where's men's brains are!
Am me right, ladies?!

Speaking of fairer sex,
ever notice when female zombie eat brains,
she sit down, but when male zombie eat brains,
he stand up?

What am up with that?

On to current events,
remember when we stormed Washington D.C.
thinking we would find brains?

Last time we did something that ironic
was when we ate George Romero's brain!

Me time almost up,
but let me know leave with this—

Me may not be the funniest zombie comic
you'll ever see—but it's un-living!

WELCOME HOME, YOU SAID
by Ronnie Stephens

I miss your knee in my ribs when I'm sleeping
and the charred waffles wafting in on Saturdays
with the tiny hymn of our daughter mixing bowl
after bowl of batter. I cannot wait to see you.

They are wrong about us, you know. We are not
dead. Hunger has hijacked our limbs.

Do you know what it is to kill against your will,
to recognize the flowers outside your home
and the door splintered open with a cannibal rage
that is not your own?

You didn't even ask why I did it.
Just held our daughter tight against your chest
and smiled. And I wish my hands
were still my hands, my eyes any eyes but mine.

FOR ONCE YOU HAVE CONQUERED DEATH, WHAT ELSE IS LEFT BUT ART?

by Stephen Meads

There is a formal element to movie-going
that makes the Zombie Gentleman feel
debonair. His jacket, single breast, slate pinstripes,
hangs loose over his ribs, hides the rotting portion of his abdomen.
His joints no longer work smooth but the stiff suit
cuts a strong figure—disguises the more extreme lurches.

The Zombie Gentleman is a Bergman fan, enjoys black and white,
        doesn't mind subtitles,
doesn't like zombie films, save the original *Night of the Living Dead*,
more like a documentary, he likes those.
Likes too, the theaters which show old movies,
the pomp of the arthouses, classic architecture,
columns, balcony seats, gold leaf, giant ornate curtains
and their tapestries, their crushed red velvet fringes at the bottom,
reminds him of blood, of what it was to be
alive, it is life-affirming; art at its finest.

The transport that is the dark
of the theater is like being buried.
The Zombie Gentleman wore a suit then too,
the jacket, stiff slate pinstripes, made him look pleasant.
When the picture starts the light feels like it did in his fist
sinking back through dirt in that first punch to the surface,
the moon poured down, taunting him,
he wanted to walk again. He defied death.
On screen a knight sits at a chessboard;
the Zombie Gentleman cannot read subtitles
but he understands the opponent, he knows
the stakes of the game. Life

may lose its feeling over time
like a corpse. It may pale
and wither. Indeed it does: each autumn
like a grave dug open, each winter
a lowered casket, each spring. . . .

The Zombie Gentleman took his first steps outside the grave gingerly,
beyond a hill loomed a hooded figure. The Zombie Gentleman overtook it
in a series of extreme lurches, his teeth made short work the flesh,
he groaned over other sounds. The figure's cloak sopped up the blood
but a little sprayed across the fringe of the Zombie Gentleman's suit.
    It wasn't enough.
He still hungered for something that would stimulate the intellect.

LOOKING THE THIEF IN THE EYE
LOOTING AFTER THE APOCALYPSE
by Nicole Homer

1.
The eyes first,
before limp and drag
or groan and mumble.
The hunger keeps house in the eyes.

They say it started in vials
in labs
in the daydreams of ambitious medical researchers.
They say it spoke its first words
sitting in plush leather at a conference table
reading a profit and loss statement
or it was straight-spined and four-starred at a war table
looking at a map and doing the math of dead men.

They say a lot of things.

It started.
How is a luxury,
a philosophical exercise,
wasted seconds one might better spend reloading.

2.
The sting. The army of teeth
sharpened against unthinking instinct.
The body can only hold so much fight.
only resist the pulling of limbs
and the pressing of canines
for so long.

The taste of it: blood
and flesh.
The bite becomes the hunger,
a thin needle,
a blunt and stabbing knife,
a banging hammer,
everything, everything, everything.

3.
You'll remember with a cynical fondness
the movies,
how slow the deadflesh walked,
the vacant stare,
the appetite,
the gray skin and rotted voice boxes.
You'll think of the directors and
you'll understand why they edit—
the utility and magic of what they leave out.
You will miss the fairytales
you were milkfed.

4.
What matters now is the eyes.
It has been a long, long afterparty.
There is no mascara left
and there so few of you fighting.

You didn't know how quickly they could turn.
You knew the basics;
sever the head, always carry your own weapon,
and blunt will do what aim cannot.

You knew human.
You knew travel in packs
but you didn't know that what was coming for you, ladies,
would still be alive
skin red and flushed ripe with adrenaline.

You knew law and punishment.
You knew judge and sentence.
You didn't know commodity and muscle mass.

You know, now, that every unchecked appetite
will plant its teeth in you and feed.
You know that hunger comes so fast
and so long before
the grumblemoandrag and gray of the beasts
you thought were the only thing hiding in the dark
and waiting for you with open mouths.

AFTER THE 2012 APOCALYPSE
by Stevie Edwards

I had a woman's voice once, too high
some said, a little too much like
an apology, but at least it wasn't this
wasting moan. I thought grotesque meant
the way my blue jeans cut into the soft skin
at my waist. I must have had good
skin. I try not to remember mornings
waking in a good light to a man with a cigarette
voice murmuring something about softness
into my hair, fingers tracing an hourglass
along my side. Someone once told me I didn't
deserve good things if I wasn't going to
appreciate them—must have been my mother.
I cut holes in new denim,
frayed hems, wanted to look less
safe. Once, I mounted my friend's horse
bareback because I wanted to know how it felt
to be thrown by something more wild
than grief. I didn't shatter any bones.
I was always mounting avoidable hazards.
I never believed that anything could end.
The applesauce in my pantry expired in 2013.
I was graduating graduate school in 2014.
Things were getting ready to happen.
I had dreams about this rotting
face. I'd shake my mother from bed,
raving that I couldn't keep my skin on.
She bought books about dreams and decided
I must need to shed something. I wish
I'd listened to the woman on the street corner
selling amulets to ward against this. I didn't
believe until a man who must've had
a name once, who was always good
with his hands, always too thin, who
I must've almost loved like hard laughter,

came rapping at my apartment door, turned
my TV on to CNN. I couldn't deny the faces.
The attack on Wrigley Field. The useless
bats, the cries of trapped fans. *We've got to
get out of the city*, he said. And we did.
He hot-wired the first vehicle with 4-wheel drive
we could find, and we headed north, headed for
woods, for a safer coast of Lake Michigan.
He said we'd be safe. He left me
on a cold night, an offering of a dead rabbit
by the fire, his last lighter still in my pocket.
I searched the shoreline for days, hoping
to find his body. It's only fair to know what
you've been left for. And then they came
and used their terrible mouths on me. I ran
for the lake and swam until my limbs
turned rot, floated to land. I stalk the coast
craving good flesh, what's been taken
from me. And I'm supposed to be grateful
because this is hunger, which is to say
I have survived as something, haven't ended.

HERE COMES THE...
by Melissa May

Because old lovers know, whatever flames
as brilliant as mid-summer sun never really dies,
that two people who once knew the combinations to
each others' secret compartments will always spark
if proximity and alcohol allow.

Because there is still a flicker of heat, no larger
than a storm-cellar candle that writes your name
on the inside of a palm that belongs to someone else.

Because in some small, annoying manner—
I will always love you.
I can only hope that the zombie apocalypse begins on your wedding day.

Please,
do not misinterpret my wish as
envy. It is not bitterness that raises fantasies
of your quaint churchyard ceremony gatecrashed by
a thousand lead-foot mockeries of your bride's descent
down the aisle.
I do not picture myself in her place.
Do not want you waiting like a sentinel for me
to shamble corpse-like to your trembling arms.

It is the only suitable gift I could conjure
for the occasion.

That your bride would assume the gasps and squeals
from the well-meaning onlookers would be ones of delight.
That when the first drooling mandible closed around her
pearl-crusted neck, she would almost mistake it for your kiss.

I can only hope the crimson faucet of her jugular will not
clash with the bouquet she has chosen. That her dress was never a cause
of debate while hammering out details, let's face it—
she shouldn't have been wearing white in the
first place.

When she turns, I pray it is not her that
you run from. It would help me sleep at night to
think you clever enough to clamor for safety. But
I know you, even through the maze of broken bodies
and the tacky slurp of satiation from long-dead appetites,
you will try to play the hero, it is
your Achilles tendon that forced me to
bury my love for you to begin with.

Apocalypse Theory #18
by Cam Awkward-Rich

Nobody can blame you
for feeling on edge
these days, as if
the whole flat span of it
will suddenly drop off
after all. The birds, thousands,
are found with lungs choked
up in their throats.

The fish, more, not even gasping.
Just wash up, already sputtered out.
In Kentucky
they are scrounging
for money
to build an ark.
For tourism. Or
just in case.

*

The human is born gill-less
and wingless, wild
for only a moment,
fists clenching
the new air.
As a child
I am already afraid of the water.
As a child
I sit up in the branches
and hold my breath
to empty myself out
to quiet my insides enough
to hear it coming.

2012: A ZOMBIE STORY
by Khary Jackson

Jan 4th, 2012

Morning, baby. I hope the Afghan air wraps your skin like me.
Keep outwitting the bullets. Only four months til the gates open and
you return to me, hell fires nipping at your boots. I dream of you
singed, ready to fall ash upon me. I have a second interview today.
Kiss me with your trigger. Write me.

Jan 16th, 2012

Baby, I don't know if you're gonna make it home so soon. A new
war, it's dragging slow and fresh, ravenous as our growing paranoia.
It's this fucking calendar, baby, these fucking Mayans scaring us all to
shit 'cause they were too lazy to extend the dates. There have been
seventeen movies about it starring Christian Bale, Bible people in
the streets shouting Revelation in my ear, even atheists are trying to
invent some kinder god to pray to. Fox News is talking about North
Korea, even India, and Obama's eyes have been looking darker and
darker. It's like everyone thinks they're running out of time to take
over the world. But maybe I'm wrong. I mean, c'mon. It's just Fox.

Mar 1st, 2012

I'm scared, baby. I haven't heard back from you since December, and
even CNN is pissing itself. They're talking about some new kind of
bomb being born, some freaky bio thing, "changing" people. The
terror alert is green...

July 9th, 2012

There was this huge cloud today. Mushroom. Everyone's faces
frozen upward . . . this is what it must have been like in Nagasaki.
Nothing happened, I just felt this tingling under my skin, cloud
vibrations crawling under. And we all went back to work, like the
sky was supposed to look like that.

August 18th, 2012

Baby, what the fuck! Animated dead people are *dashing on air,* flying and dicing, hinge-less jaws crunching into heads! The TVs and radios are dead, the mail man was slaughtered last week, so how the fuck will you read this?? My own body twitches and shifts. And my mind, sometimes…

September 29th, 2012

Please, if you're alive, do not come. I'm so sorry, baby…I killed someone today. Some boy scout, howling, my claws wouldn't stop. My laser eyes blazed his stomach, my snaking hair constricting his throat. His heart was peach and sugar…*how do zombies even have lasers?*

December 29nd, 2012

According to that fucking calendar, the planet should have chewed us into dust a week ago. Nothing has happened. We're eating ourselves. No one here is still alive to swallow, so I found the closest thing. I'm eating our pictures, baby…washing them down with the frames and glass. All the silk you left me, the strands of hair, the pictures of the ultrasound before we lost her. Will anyone remember us, baby? How once we were lovely? Tell them…please…my name …was Kh…

ZOMBIE (1994)
by Lindsay Eanet

It's the ominous haze of the first chord
then the roar of the bar patrons.
I will never understand
how The Cranberries' "Zombie" became
our arms-around-each-other swaying
inebriated, sweaty braying
karaoke skill displaying
anthem of choice.

Nostalgia, perhaps. Memories of
alternative radio after Kurt Cobain
but before the Napster Revolution
when radio still held our attention.
Or the mention of zombies, the catchy
chorus.
The fact that yodeling is fun.
The macabre juxtaposition of our glee
over this communal breaking into song
with the darkness and destruction
its lyrics convey.
The all too real and recent struggles
of a fractured island.

Even here in the north of England
within a breath of the site
of the Warrington bombings that compelled
Dolores O'Riordan and her band to turn weeping and wailing
into gnashing of guitars
surrounded by Northern Irish transplants
and posh Oxford boys that know
every word to "Come Out Ye Black And Tans"
and "The Man Behind the Wire"
yowling with exaggerated brogues
relish each syllable of "Zombie"
rolling around each of Dolores's gasps and shrieks in their mouths
like fragile grapes or pomegranates

inviting the whole room into the fraternity of the chorus
while cans of Carlsberg litter the living room floor.

I have a friend in Liverpool
whose grandmother was gunned down by
Loyalist paramilitary forces in Belfast.
Over pints we trade stories and histories
family legacies marred by death squads and death camps
and compare tattoos—ours were etched in skin by choice
some of my family's were not.

We always end up talking about religion,
and I think it's because
we understand what it's like
to be recounted your history on repeat
and told "This is what you are"—to have a relationship with God
because the absence of God means submitting
to those who have wronged you
to walk with the dead always
several steps behind.

Sarah's mother still watches BBC specials
about the Shankill Butchers.
The closest experience I had was being made
to watch *The Sound of Music* every year around Christmastime:
enraptured with solid-bodied, silver-voiced Rolf
a kinder, gentler form of fascism.
Oppression that teaches you the waltz first.

Remember that zombies
always start out
as human beings.

I read somewhere
that the only way to evade zombies
is by crossing a large body of water
and so our grandparents and parents
and the hundreds of thousands from everywhere like them
fled the grasp of the undead on boats to England,
America, Canada, Palestine, everywhere and anywhere.

So Fela Kuti fled his Nigeria
sailed across the water to America
to escape the ghosts of fellow revolutionaries
whose death-groans haunted him
only to come back
and record his full assault
on the zombie army which had taken over his beloved nation.

As the record flips over
from one "Zombie"
to the other
and back again
our enemy recontextualized and repackaged and sold as sequels
to bring up old enemies encased in our memories
so do we prepare to battle our zombies another way
through recognizing the human flesh
underneath rotting, pallid exteriors
choose to reconcile with the unfamiliar
teach it to waltz
to play guitar
maybe to love.

As the horde closes in
we will go down singing.

SEXY ZOMBIE HAIKU #1
by Megan Thoma

I will eat your brains.
Best way to brains is to go
through your vagina.

Nancy's First Kill
by Raundi Moore-Kondo

Nancy wasn't home early from visiting her mother she was just in time for lunch. She didn't recall being married to Ted but she could still smell another woman's brains on his lips from 3 blocks away. CNN's live coverage of the spreading invasion blared from their only working television. It ran 24/7 in the bunker that once behaved like a living room. Nancy only heard the moans coming from the kitchen. W-D40 and cosmoline did nothing to dilute the gnawing pungency of flesh devouring flesh. Of blood and perspiration spiked with serotonin and endorphins. Of euphoric brains running hot on friction induced adrenaline.

Ted, a former card-carrying member of the hair club for men, was naked, bare back to the door, a half-loaded .22 by his side. The poster child for erectile dysfunction had just taken his last black-market little blue pill and was finally prepared to defile his secretary sprawled out over the breakfast table. A former stock photo model, she'd been product placement for crossbows and subliminal advertising for vacuum therapy pumps.

There was no malice in Nancy's movements. She didn't hate the secretary. There was no anger to fatten or rage to offset her newly acquired stagger. She couldn't fathom a scorned housewife's jealousy. Only a day ago she'd been the epitome of pearl necklace pity. Today, she was just hungry. She didn't need to be swift or understand the element of surprise. Ted's dictation taker was a screamer. They never heard Nancy coming.

Her excommunicated catholic knees genuflected into Ted's ribcage, crushing both clavicles and robbing the last Hail Mary from his collapsing lungs. The very heels that had maxed out his credit punctured his overburdened kidneys. Two manicured nails plucked the apple from his throat to silence the whistle spitting from his panicked larynx. She gripped the hair at the base of his recently plugged scalp to survey the full landscape of his neck. Then cracked him open like his skull came stock with flip-top. Her teeth tore sinew from bone and popped cartilage from connective tissue exposing the most delicate vertebrae his limp spine had to offer. Nancy craved warm bone marrow as much as throbbing brain matter but she still couldn't stomach his heart.

The un-wanton whimpers of the secretary buried under Ted's belly were a reminder to save room for dessert. A terrorized face trapped beneath the sweat-covered shoulder of her mostly dead employer. Her powdered cheek lay in a pool of his blood. She was stock photo of angel food cake in raspberry sauce. Two courses for the price of one; the best three-way Nancy ever had.

VISCERAL LOVE
by Sean O' Neil

Wait . . .
After you go quiet,
I recognize you.
Like the sweet smell
of a spilled viscus
slowly sizzling on the noonish asphalt,
I remember happy cookouts
in far-off, smiling times.
And gazing deep into your glazed eyes,
you make me feel so vaguely alive.
And even as I savagely scrape and claw
each sticky morsel
from your brain-pan's dorsal wall.
I pretend I can just barely hear the trickle
of a tiny tear
as it rolls down
and tickles
my half-eaten face.
Such was my love for you.

ZOMBIE CLASSIFIEDS
by Paul Suntup

GUARANTEED DECAPITATION PREVENTION
Our patented Zombie Neck Brace is
constructed using reinforced steel rebar.
Guaranteed to prevent decapitation by chainsaw
or your money back.
Call our toll-free number today.
Free overnight shipping.

PLUMP HUMAN DELIVERY SERVICE
Tired of prowling the streets looking for humans to eat?
Let us bring them right to your doorstep!
We can deliver as few as one human, or as many as fifty.
Call now to schedule your first order.
Subscription service available.

SLOW THE DECOMPOSITION PROCESS
Feel disgusted when you look in the mirror?
Tired of waking up with pieces of your face
missing? Now you can do something about it with
our unique Anti-Decaying Night Crème.
Apply generously once a day to affected areas.
Visible results within 5 days.

ZELDA'S NAIL & BEAUTY SPA
Clawing endlessly at wooden doors to get at your
afternoon snack can wreak havoc with your fingernails.
Come to Zelda's for a full makeover!
We specialize in zombie manicures.
This month's special: half price on a full set of
spiked acrylic nails.

ZOMBIE SUPPORT GROUP
We have helped thousands of zombies deal with
depression. Are you experiencing feelings of hopelessness
related to your inevitable decomposition?
Has all the fun gone out of eating brains?

We can help! Call us now for a free consultation. Mention this ad and get a complimentary tube of Anti-Decaying Night Crème.

Theme from Bobby's Sitcom
by Jennifer Gigantino

Bobby wakes up every morning
and forgets about the boards nailed
behind the Venetian blinds. He's got

a sarcastic oil painting of indeterminate
vintage (which cracks wise and British at
the expense of Bobby's hygiene or lack

thereof). He's got a tube sock that can
stand up by itself. He's got the Tao
of Bob Saget and problems that solve

themselves in half an hour. He's got
thick apartment walls between him and
the rest of the world. He's got stopped

clocks and eight o'clock (seven central)
forever. He's got a guest appearance
by John Stamos, or maybe not. He knows

how to build a bomb. He knows how
to bathe in moldy coffee grounds and
wash his hair with formaldehyde. He

knows how to stand as still as the end
of the world when he hears those things
groaning outside. He knows that if
you listen for long enough, any white
noise can sound like a laugh track.

THE PUG AND I MISS YOU. COME HOME.
by Bucky Sinister

1

It was supposed to be simple;
you were going on tour
leaving the pug with me
and you would be back in two months.

Then came the zombies.

It was horrible,
like we always imagined,
as the movies and comic books predicted,
and eventually it was over.

In a couple of weeks,
the whole world became complicated.
You were supposed to be back a week ago.

Waiting is worse than a zombie attack.

2

I walk the pug several times a day,
still carrying a shotgun and a propane torch,
just in case.

After the zombies finally gave out and died,
Oakland was filled with flies like you wouldn't believe.
The flies were followed by the frogs and birds.
The smell is overwhelming,
rotten zombies and birdshit.

The pug doesn't seem to mind.
In fact, he seems to be cataloguing all the bodies
for some kind of doggie diary.

The pug and I go around the lake, usually,
where I've burned most of the bodies but there's a stench
coming off the lake that I don't know how to fix.

The heartbreaking part is when we get home,
he always looks to see if you're there.

3

When the shit was going down,
I was conscripted into the military,
when they came through and found out I could shoot.
There's always room in the army
for a country boy
who's good with a rifle.

When they pulled out,
they let me keep the M24 Remington.

I camped out with the pug
on the roof of the building
across from Mama Buzz
and shot the last remaining
hipster zombies
as they straggled
with their vestigial memories
for a cup of coffee.

That's when I saw the ex,
the one who told me
she was moving to Portland
and never did.

Through the scope,
I watched her lope up the sidewalk
with her feather earrings,
art portfolio under her arm.
I took the shot.
Closure.

4

If you're reading this,
come down to the Tribune building.
That's where we live now.

I hope the two stops of the tour
were good for you.

I hope you sold a lot of books.
The world needs books
now more than ever.

Fuck, I hope you're alive.
The pug believes you are,
and I trust him.

"Word Problems of the Day" or "Why I Was Asked to Stop Teaching Math"

by Tim Stafford

1

Johnny has run away from the zombies. The zombie horde is moving at a constant rate of .25 miles per hour. If Johnny's shelter is 3.5 miles away, how long will it take the horde to reach him?

2

Tommy needs to board up the first floor windows of his shelter. There are 5 windows and each of them requires 3 boards. If each board needs 4 nails and it takes 20 seconds per nail, how long will it take Tommy to board up all 5 windows?

3

Debbie lives in an apartment complex with 40 units. If 60% of the units are infected with the walking dead, how many apartments are NOT infected?

4

Dionte has been keeping track of how many zombies have stumbled past his hideout each day. Over the past four days there were 65, 53, 32, and 44. On average, how many zombies stumble past Dionte's hideout?

Answers: 1) 16 hours 2) 1200 sec or 20 min 3) 16 units 4) 48.5 zombies

SEPARATION ANXIETY
by Rob Sturma

There was talk, subdued gossip
neighbor talk, safe behind fence,
about my commitment to the Cause.

I was never one of those diehards,
the ones who placed the severed heads
on stakes in the front yard, a tally of
how many flesh-eaters they'd personally
taken out. Mr. Hucklebee, the accountant
two houses down, was the quietest before
his oldest daughter came to visit,
swaddled in a sanguine jacket with
shaken toddlers in tow. Didn't take but a day
before their pupils were glazed over with
the milky film glaucoma look that we all
came to know as Zombie Eye. Hucklebee
had no choice but to pick up an axe
and do the math.

Those were his first three heads.

Placed on his lawn, neat and in a row,
soon followed by trophies from around the
neighborhood. The mailman had been
shambling up and down the cul-de-sac
for a week prior, and no one had put him
down until Ol' Hucklebucket and his
double barrel signed, sealed, and delivered the
disgruntled bitebeast.   The foxy PTA mom
had a conference with a crossbow.
On and on, Huckles found his inner
Cimmerian, and soon the garden gnomes
were replaced with a display that looked
for all the world like a twisted giant Pez
collection.

I was never one for accolades; any old
spelling bee trophies were thrown to the
wayside years ago. My sense of
competition is next to nil. It doesn't make
me a better person to show off my kills,
my scalps, to show how big my
survivor shotgun is.

There are no head-sicles adorning
my freshly mowed grass. Just a few
spots of sullied dirt in the back. One,
large and long, for my lover's body.
The other, no bigger than a breadbox,
for her beautiful, transformed, milky

skull.

I HATE ZOMBIES LIKE YOU HATE ME
by Scott Woods

Here is what I wish would happen:
a windy November day,
before the snow has spilled its milk
and the leaves still grip the ground in their stiff handshakes,
that while visiting your grandmother's gravesite,
having cleared away the autumn debris and dew dust,
I wish your grandmother would break the crust
and reach for you,
swirl her knobby, apple-pie baking bones around your ankle
and drag herself out of the trench she has been digging,
staring at you with unblinking, puss-laden eyes
yellow from a lack of sun and birthdays,
baring her teeth at your snot-nosed five-year-old who only
wants to know if you're going to stop at
McDonald's on the way home.

I wish that in that mortifying moment you
remember how, while we sat in a theater
and the trailer for yet another zombie movie splayed across
the cinema canvas, you turned to me and said,
"Zombies are awesome."
And when I said "I am so sick of zombies,"
you decided then and there that you
would never attend a third date.

I wish that your grandmother was followed by another grandmother,
and another, and a jawless uncle who lost his way after the war.

And because it's Veterans Day he will be a wily zombie general,
and his moans will mean a thing,
and on his one-armed, jawless command
every grave with a flag spits forth the contents of their dingy bellies
and the zombie invasion begins,
right there,
where you are,
while you try to remember
what was so cool about them in the first place.

It used to be vampires;
so fine, so literate, so thin and grazed of chin.
You used to coo over them, too; pecked at
every book featuring a woman too abundant for corsets,
two red dents of ancient love dotting her pristine neck.
Lame.
Even you would have to admit that just because you've been
bitten in the neck wouldn't make you a better lover.
You would still be as ugly as you ever were.
You'd just be ugly longer.

If we are honest, we do not love the zombie.
We do not think the zombie is cool.
We do not imagine the zombie for a lover or a count or a
Tom Cruise/Brad Pitt sandwich.
All zombie stories are about us,
about the people who aren't zombies,
and how we scream and run and die when something
without the brain God gave a snow globe
somehow manages to destroy us in a shopping mall.
So all zombie stories are about autumn and brains and
shopping carts and whatever else we can throw in their shambling path
to make the un-cool undead hooligan cool again.

So here is what I wish would happen:
that next Veteran's Day,
when you go visit the grave of your
stoic and cigar-munching grandfather
that you think about the fact that I bought the popcorn
and the tickets
and the Gummi Bears you let fall through the seat and shrugged at,
like they didn't cost shit.
And you remember,
when Gramps is chompin' at the bit from underneath you,
his Purple Heart swinging from the ventricles of his purple heart,
that I was a good man
you let slip through your fingers.

CLEAVER
by Dain Michael Down

There is a meat cleaver.
It was not purchased, nor will it ever be used, for its intended purpose.
It is cleaned to shine almost obsessively;
a warm breath and a dish rag will do the job.

It's a novelty, really,
but the idea that it could be used against an intruder is comforting.
Whether it be a junkie looking for their fix
or a zombie, looking for their fix.

It might come in handy.
It hangs on a hook for easy access,
but it is only useful if there is strength behind the blade.

Should a zombie enter your residence,
take hold of the cleaver in your dominant hand with a tight grip.

From an elevated position, bring the cleaver down,
aiming for the crux of the neck and shoulder, angling the blade in
        towards the base of the skull.
The adrenaline should allow for a complete severing of the spine.

When the zombie falls to its knees,
place foot to chest and pull cleaver out.
If there is another zombie, raise cleaver above head
and repeat.

If this is, in fact, the zombie apocalypse,
a cleaver is not the best choice for your defense.
But if it is just a random outbreak, you should fare well as long as you
        are properly rested.
I suggest you invest in a machete today.

Knife-Depot.com has the "Trademark Colossal 25 inch Heavy Duty
        Machete" with a nylon sheath for just $21.49 and it is listed as
        HOT!

That means place your order today so you will not be left out when
the waves of undead are pouring through your front door.

Guns are A-OK if you're a good shot.
If not, you'll just be making the zombies heavier with all that lead.
Invest in a good pair of running shoes.
Start exercising.

Staying in one place is foolish.
Travel in packs.
Do not hesitate to kill your mother should she start to turn.

In fact, nip it in the bud—
if she gets so much as a paper cut,
raise cleaver, or newly purchased machete above head
and bring it down with love.
With force, but with love.
She will thank you in the zombie afterlife
you are inevitably going to meet her in.
Because, let's be honest.
Running away
is really just delaying the inevitable.

ZOMBIE LOVE SONG
by Laura Yes Yes

Today, in the carelessness of noon, my lover asked me,
Would you still love me if I were a zombie?

I see. Our relationship has reached the point
where I need to be thinking about the future.

What kind of zombie are we talking about?
A Haitian zombie? Is he doing someone else's bidding?
Could I cure him by giving him salt?

That's pretty unlikely, though.
I have to assume he'd be the standard brand of undead.
When we're fooling around on the couch
and he's nibbling on my neck,
innocent as a lamb at pasture,

it all goes suddenly, horribly wrong,
his canines tearing deep into my flesh,
nails clawing wildly at the inconvenience of my skull.

He doesn't know.

I was trained to decapitate a man
at a thousand paces with a single shotgun shell.
I'm well-versed in the science of a machete's arc,
and don't test me on the heft of a Louisville Slugger.
I keep a Shaolin spade tucked under my mattress
for the instant a good man goes wrong.

But in the gold of today, I find myself considering
the miracle of knots. Clinch knots, figure eights,
palomars, wondering which would bind him best.
What would help with the smell once he really begins to decay?
Incense? Febreze?

Perhaps most importantly, can a zombie give consent?

I do know one thing, at least.
I take in my hands two locks of hair
and offer as answer a blood knot.
This is my way of saying:

My star, I will never let you eat my brains.
But if you wish, I'll carry you into the life
beyond life, beyond usefulness and logic.
I will hold you close
until you irredeemably decompose—

unless, of course, you're one of those fast zombies,
in which case I adore you, my darling, my dear,
and I've got a shotgun shell with your name all over it.

LIKE MY SEX (UNDEAD EDITION)
by Omar "Ion" Holmon

zombie girlfriend, when you swallow, it leaks
like a broken piñata

ZOMBIE
by Daniel McGinn

You attractive, like flower.
You bleed, like honey.

Zombie stagger in swarm,
like narcoleptic bee.
Zombie sting you.
Zombie help you die.

Zombie had roots, roots are broken.
Zombie have brains, full of desire.
Zombie love brains, brains for dinner.

Child's hand lets go of balloon.
Balloon sails farther and farther away,
balloon is no longer visible.
Balloon is gone forever.
The child cries, or the child doesn't cry.
It doesn't matter anymore.

Zombie is like that.
Zombie strong, like rot.
Zombie jaws are terrible.
Zombie do not bathe.

Zombie pounce.
Skull cap pops.
Red child drops.

Zombie get down on that.
Zombie reproduce.
Zombie rise and walk.
Zombie stumble and fall.

THE ZOMBIE, REJECTED BY HIS HUMAN LOVER, RESPONDS (FOR MEGAN THOMA)

by John Paul Davis

I'm writing this with my finger,
dipped in the pulp
of my own clotting blood
on the concrete
wall of a parking garage.
The air was a blurry
headache the night
I first saw you,
skin aglow like starlight
on a sidewalk,
some candle
I lack irradiating
the stained-glass sea
in your eyes.
I don't remember what bite
or voodoo narrowed
me to this undying season
of wanting. I only
know I'm hunger. I'd swallow
myself if I could.
I can feel myself
decomposing. I shake,
and shake.
I'm an orchestra of lurches,
a spell of falling,
I couldn't help but tilt
toward you, but what amazed
my wilting mind
was that you saw
the telltale angle
of my stumble,
heard the primal
deep of my smeared

excuse for language.
You knew what
I was and took
me home anyway.
In this I might be no
different than any man.
Here is something no
other human knows:
every night in the sting
of cool right before dawn
we gather, all over,
a rotting congregation.
Some compass
in us inclines
our faces toward Pluto,
and we will turn
toward it as one
and hum a graveled,
shivering hymn.
It has no words.
Last night I shuffled
not to the pallid
rooftop where we gather
but wavered
outside your window
as you slept and sang,
not to the underworld,
but to you. I'm
in orbit around something
new. I'm now something
other than what my body
demands of me. Sweet,
I love you for more
than your brain.
What other man
has ever said that?

THE THING ABOUT HAVING
JUST DROPPED ACID AN HOUR AGO
WHEN THE ZOMBIES ARRIVE
AT THE HOUSE PARTY
by Mindy Nettifee

is that you know with total certainty you are doomed.
You could run wind sprints down the ribboning post-suburban streets,
scale fences and bougainvillead stucco, crouch on shoddy rooftops,
but you will not just be defenseless sometime in the next thirty minutes,
you will be epically defenseless, vulnerable to loud wallpaper.
Furthermore, that thirty minutes could last an entire year, and not
        just any year,
an adolescent year, the kind spent sweating out enough ripened hormones
to halt the menopause of a whole Sweet Adelines convention.
The zombies will definitely get you.

As the LSD begins to catch its diamond-webbed footing
in the cat's cradle of your synapses, your fear cranks into curiosity,
and your curiosity sharply blossoms into some full-bodied vodka of yes.
There is screaming, but also some of the sweetest garage rock
you've heard in a long time charging out of the stereo,
and maybe it's just you—wait, it's totally just you—
but the screaming has become a tight rehearsed punk chorus.
The living room is forced and vivid and pulsing, and it all starts
to synchronize with these gorgeous arcs of glittering blood and brains.

Holy fuck, the glittering! Like everything is just a mirror of a mirror,
a shattering of a shattering, like all theses living bodies had just
been waiting all along to burst into disco balls of death song.
When the tallest zombie turns and lurches toward you,
you can't help but fixate on the decomposed canary lining of his
        funeral suit.
It contrasts against his rotting skin which looks like it's been studying worms
who studied crickets who studied the death of the novels written by
        night stars.
His eyes shine like a dog's.

He grabs clumsily at you, and the trip is really spinning its God wheels now,
and you think you should lower your head like an offering.
Instead, you look him straight in his undead eyes and say,
"Let's go, this party's dead," and laugh like a drunk kid.
Then, "It's ok, man, it's all connected.
It's all conn—

BARBARA
by Wonder Dave

At first you ran, stumbled, broke
the heel of your shoe.

The car wouldn't start;
you were in distress, weren't you, damsel;

catatonic on the couch haunted by your brother's
eyes. When he broke through

the barriers, arms outstretched, how
could you not reach back?

You did everything a woman should.
You let yourself be devoured.

An Open Letter
to the University of Florida
by AJ Moyer

Dear whomever at the University of Florida
happens to open this letter:

We will remember this when they are eating our brains,
that is, if they haven't already eaten the part for remembering
how the university board thought a Zombie Survival Guide
on the university's health department web page was degrading.

Of course health threats must be taken seriously,
and knowing about vaccines and safe sex is important,
especially in college,

but to think that these lessons are cheapened
by posting a document that could literally save our brains
from reanimated corpses that want nothing more
than to eat us where we stand,

that's just hodgepodge.
That's fucking horsefeathers,
University of Florida;
sheer and utter poppycock.

We can study viruses and safe sex,
we can develop vaccines in labs and
treatments for other sorts of infection,
the health department hands out enough condoms,
but all we had to save us from the undead
is that pamphlet you've taken down.
We'll never have a chance to study them
until it is too late.

Zombie survival pop quiz, oh person
at the University of Florida
who happened to open my letter:
Where do you go to hide in a zombie apocalypse?

The Mall? The University? Home?
Congratulations, you're fucked.
Just like your students are since you took down that guide!

How can we be expected to stay safe
and be prepared for our adult lives
when you have the gall to deny us
necessary health resources.

It's a safety issue, really.

Zombie survival pop quiz number 2:
What is the optimum number of people
to have in your survival party?

Number 3:
What are the most important skills to have
in the aftermath of a zombie apocalypse?

Number 4:
How do you balance the survival of your new clan
with your food and weaponry resources?

Number 5:
Where do you tell your students to go
when Urban Meyer stumbles off the football field
with half a cheerleader's jugular in his teeth?

If you can't answer that, oh person
at the University of Florida
who happened to read this letter,
then approximately 51,000 students
whose families have entrusted you and yours
with their lives are now going to die!

For the sake of your students,
oh person at the University of Florida,
please pass this letter to your superiors,
ask the medical department to hold hearings,
because if you think sexually transmitted infections
and drugs are all we have to worry about in college,

it's time you realized we could use some awareness
about all the mindless stumblers out there
wanting nothing more than to desecrate our brains.

Please, person at Florida,
make them reconsider
protecting our brains.

FEAR AND EMBRACE
by Hugh Pham

Kiss me before another mouth finds you,
one without lips, blood crusted, and gray.
Remind me how living is more than a pulse
when still hearts hunger a mile away.
Let's make love in our well-hidden nest,
grappling repressed phantoms to make us warm.
But carefully caress, not claw or hack,
like humanoid clouds of the shuffling storm.
I'll avoid those marauding thoughts of you,
those blue eyes crimson, your veins, varicose
with violet violence and craving;
these days, we quietly fear loved ones most.
Hold tightly, the voracious dead won't tear
a cell of your spirit while I'm here.

When you tell her about it,
assure her it's no big deal.
It's just a thing.
Everybody has a thing.
You have a thing, I have a thing,
but really you feel fine.

10 Things You Didn't Know About Being a Zombie
by Chad Anderson

One.
When you first get bit,
when you feel the lesion scarring its inevitable into you,
you want to tell everyone;
old friends, ex-lovers, people who held some insignificance against you.
"Really sorry to hear you're a zombie now.
We should have lunch."
You decide not to say a word.
You have a secret now
and you'll take it to the grave.

Two.
It's not like the movies.
Sure, there are some good examples
but they never get it just right.
You can count on the fever, the moaning, the cold fingers
but that's just the body trying to alleviate,
trying to hold on to a few more moments of normal.

Three.
You've acquired a new set of friends.
There are zombie support groups, zombie online networks,
even a zombie walk in various cities throughout the year.
Every friend you know
has a friend who has a cousin who just found out they were a zombie too!
"You two should meet."

Four.
You still like all the same things;
still enjoy ice cream, still love skateboarding,
still like masturbating on the couch
when you think your roommates are asleep.
But now you have a new set of zombie priorities.
You tell yourself if you resist these things
you might live longer.

Five.
You still think about things.
You're not just some mindless monster.
You think about things all the time;
things you never thought about before;
things that keep you awake at night.
It's all the thinking you do
that keeps you from feeling.

Six.
You can still fall in love.
People never think about zombies in love, but it comes to you.
It hits you in the face like a baseball bat;
rattles in your skull like a bullet.
There is no more textbook definition of "unconditional"
than the girl who will offer up her heart
knowing exactly what you'll do with it.

Seven.
The nighttime is your ally.
When it's time to start feeding,
you need to learn to move in the darkness;
how to slip in and out of the shadows.
There will be other monsters out there
who want what you have
and if you want to keep somebody around
you keep them in the dark forever.

Eight.
You need to learn to run.
It's no time for the 1950's pace and groan.
There is a healthy life running away from you
and you need to chase it.
You need to devour it with your teeth
because time is fleeting
and some days
you can still taste it.

Nine.
There is no cure.
Even your immune system has turned against you.
But it's okay.
It's just a thing.
I mean, everybody has a thing.
You have a thing, I have a thing.
But my thing is a zombie
living inside me and eating my brain
and it scares me to death
because really,
I feel fine.

Ten.
If she doesn't run screaming
the moment you tell her,
it's already too late.

How to Be a Zombie
by Rick Lupert

Forget about the little things.
Now it is only brain
or no brain.
Always be on the lookout for fresh brain.
When no brain is present, try wandering the streets
saying the word brain over and over.
You will meet others who agree with you.
You will know them by their smell and
because they will also be saying brain.
There will be a discordant harmony to your voices.
Resist the urge to start a barbershop quartet.
Even the living won't be interested.
You may have once loved self-serve frozen yogurt
but now you won't be able to operate the levers.
Let the boy behind the counter do it for you.
Then eat his brain.
This is the last shirt you will ever wear.
Don't let the others pull it off you
in the struggle for brain.
Laundry is a concept from your past.
You don't even know what it is anymore.
Get used to walking.
They don't issue licenses to your kind.
There is no special training program and
you'd only eat the DMV employee
when it was your turn in line.
Not that you have anywhere special to be.
Destination based movement is not a priority
for you. Move on or don't. Whatever.
I do not recommend attempting to make a soufflé.
The stiffening of the egg whites requires a patience
you no longer possess. Brains are just as good
right out of the head as they would be in a pie.
Do not eat the dead.
It goes against your personal code

and tastes like shit.
When you run into the living
they will try to hurt you.
They will want to make holes in you.
They will want to make your head
go away from your body.
Avoid this.
When you run into people you knew
it won't matter. You won't remember them.
They may try to reason with you.
Pause for a moment.
Then eat their brains.
Eat their brains *so much*.

PERSPECTIVE
by Tapestry

You,
carriers of a pulse
and sweet warm tasty flesh,
I say this in your living tongue
as you do not understand my dead one.
We are your end,
demons clothed in your dead flesh.
We know not why the grave
refused us,
all we know is hunger.
You ridicule our shambling steps,
vacant gaze, and rotting skin,
but know you will never be safe.
We smell your fear,
feel the warmth of your living flesh.
We will always find you.
Comfort yourselves with your guns and explosives,
hide behind your barricades,
but we will eventually get in
and your flesh will warm our cold dead bellies,
and those not consumed
will become one of us.
You have wasted this planet for too long.
Your time here is done.
This world is ours now,
graveyard dust and shuffling corpses,
the end is ours to claim.

SEXY ZOMBIE HAIKU #2
by Megan Thoma

Let's play zombie sex
game. You eat. I'll moan. We both
feel nothing inside.

WHAT NIETZSCHE SAID
by Sam LaMura

i.
the first time she said hallelujah
    a dead dog
   fell from her mouth

    I tried to bury the dog
but it bit off my hand
      so I killed it again and

thus she spoke it once more, hallelujah

ii.
I found a knife
in my back

pulled it out slowly so I could
hear the metal grind

from the sound I could tell
it was serrated,
like a good knife should be

iii.
the dog's rotting mass has me
    thinking about
    going back to church
to drink the holy water

iv.
if Nietzsche was right
then we were the ones
created in God's image

THE SHOTGUN WAS JUST A MISUNDERSTANDING
by Adrian Wyatt

You came hurling though the chain-link fence like a student film.
Rigid as a suicidal pigeon.
You cracked your face into mine
like a mudslide through a windshield.

We crossed plot lines in the street.

I heard your minions unraveling like an armada of cleaved peacocks,
wrecked fisher-cats strangled bull horns in the suburbs.
I ran like hell
until your desire to devour me whole
stopped me dead in my tracks.

Doubled over on the concrete,
spooning in the syrup.
It clumped like crude from the gash of your mouth
and you kissed me cold.
I hummed to your bone saw sonata
as you tried scrape open my skull
the muskrat cathedrals of your teeth.
I asked you again.

"What is it about *me*
that makes you want me so much?"
You said:

BRRRRAAAAIIIIIIIIINNNNNSSSSS!!!!!

You know? I have always wanted to be loved for my intelligence
and it is *so nice* to *finally* meet a man with his priorities in order.

You plunged face-first into the muck of me.
Your exposed phalanges
war-torn and naked
from trying to claw into the depths
to find what makes me tick.

Most guys don't even *ask*.

My girlfriends won't listen to me when I tell them
that you are not using me for my body.
When I said I thought I was fat?
You tore my thigh clean off the bone.
That was really romantic.

I'm sorry I screamed.
Twitching in an oozing heap
You garbled my rebellion with a kiss
so deep to my throat
it crushed my trachea with a wood-chipper hush.

We colored the ground like a black-tie affair,
only our velvet poured out.

In the high-noon glare
I glistened under your three o'clock shadow
until you gnawed away
at every memory
of any man who came before you
and had the audacity to ask for seconds.

EMPTY NEST SYNDROME
by Grae Rose

It's never fair for a mother to
have to push a lesson onto her
child before they are ready,
but sometimes life forces us
to grow up too fast.

In the new world, family is dangerous.
The youngest will grow up knowing this,
because they will see how quickly
arbitrary kinships can lead to risky
obligations, but for those of us who
were old enough to witness the rise
of the zombie legion, who listened to
the media panic, crackle, and break down
as the virus began to spread, to swipe its
yellowed fingers across our population,
we know what it is like to value people
for more than just their skill set.
This is what makes it hardest for us.

My first child was too far for me to
protect her, holed up in a dorm room
with a thousand girls every bit as
vulnerable as she must have been.
This was before the shelters, before
we knew how to defend ourselves.
But losing one child is enough to
shock your maternal instincts into
drive, and shielding my son from the
new horrors the world had invented to
throw at us became my only concern.

Of course, in a time of war, your back
can never be placed as firmly against the
corner as you want it to be, and you are
never as protected as you think you are.
Life has a way of making sure you know

just how feeble your goals are before it
smashes them into bits, and before long
it was made clear to me that in fighting
for my son's life, I had left myself an
open target to the universe's irony.

Sometimes it seems like playing hide and seek with life and death is a
    game that only the undead can win.

So when I became infected, I shouldn't
have let it affect me the way it did.
I should have been grateful that I had
someone by my side to shut me down
before I turned, before my metamorphosis
consumed the context of my humanity.

Still, it hardly seems like yesterday that
I was teaching my son how to deal with
the death of his first pet, and now I am
faced with the task of teaching him
how to kill, how to reach beyond the
bonds of familial affinity I had so
selfishly forged to keep him by my side,
as if I could shield him from the apocalypse
as easily as I once did from the monsters
that crept beneath his bed or scratched
at his window during a thunderstorm.

It does not matter who is responsible
for the beginning of this nightmare,
because there are enough of us left
to raise the dawn and cast out the
shadows tattooed under our tired eyes.
I can only pray that my son will be
among the survivors, that he will live
past the terrors of his adolescence and
into the promise that tomorrow holds
like a flare to inspire these stragglers.
I knew there would come a time when
my baby bird would have to dive from the
sanctuary of the nest I wove around us.

My only regret is that I will never have
the chance to see him rise above and fly.

TEENAGE ZOMBIES
by Big Mike

Sleepwalking through school,
constantly late for homeroom,
feasting on Doritos and Red Bulls for breakfast.

NO DOLLAR MENU is SAFE
from these opinionated with no opinion
pimple-faced demons!

They are mindless.
They are inarticulate.
They are inconsiderate rude little bitches

with tainted tongues that speak in an
"um...like...um...errr...you know what I'm sayin..."
code only they can decipher.

They are abrasive. They are perplexing.
They are teenage fucking zombies,
know-nothing -at-all pains in the ass
in search of immediate gratification and peer acceptance.
Illiterate.

They command the internet using Umbrella Corporations,
making shorter words longer, turning letters to numbers,
phrases into acronyms to post status updates
in THIS broken English virus infecting millions.

Learn to spell, you teenage fuckin' zombie!
This shit ain't LOL, teenage fuckin' zombie
possessed by puberty.

Using cameras as weapons, snapping profile pics
in off-the-wall positions like
click.
It's not cool to post pictures of your abs,
STUPID TEENAGE ZOMBIE!
You ain't the Situation, bitch,
you VAIN teenage zombie!

These simpletons been Snookified—
looking for rude boys in perpetual heat
so they can brag about "the way they ride it"
and right after her sweet 16
she becomes a mom with a brand new baby in her arms.

Whatcha gonna do now, you horny teenage zombie?
Put the dick down! You promiscuous teenage zombie!

Lack of respect has reached epidemic proportions.
No mall, no movie theater, no Planned Parenthood is safe
from these thugged out, emo, superficial, preppy, gothic, moronic
    teenage zombies.

Parents, teachers, Al Sharpton,
gather; gather with me in libraries, museums,
and Shop Rite's produce isle!
We'll arm ourselves with belts, and books.

Whap! Pick your pants up, teenage zombie!
We're tired of seeing the crack of your ass, teenage zombie!
Using dictionaries and thesauruses to bash in skulls
until complete sentences are spoken.

We will sever their lifelines...
by building skinny jean bonfires,
donate their Xboxes,
fuck your Halo online!
Cut their cell phones off.
Get your own damn phone plan, teenage zombie!

Buy your own cereal,
cook your own meals,
get your own La-Z-Boy recliner,
pay some fuckin' rent, you freeloading-ass zombie

Despite what Will Smith has led you to believe
in this house . . . I am Legend!

My name is Michael Bertram.
I am a surviving parent living in New Jersey.
I am broadcasting on all AM frequencies
because all these little sum-bitches do
is listen to their iPod touches.

I will be at the Chinese Buffet, EVERYDAY, at mid-day,
when the sun is highest in the sky.

If you are out there, if anyone is out there,
I can provide buffalo wings and beer.
I can provide shelter with a 52-inch HDTV,
I can provide a cure to this plague
that involves whooping some teenage zombie ass.
If there's anybody out there…anybody…join me!
You are not alone!

NIGHT OF THE LIVING
by Steve Ramirez

I used to believe my father was a zombie.

Mom would wake us to the dawn of another day without dad,
and we'd search the parking lots of the local zombie discotecas.

Once, we found him in the torn leather interior of our Ford Falcon,
asleep in an alley two blocks away, engine still running.

Other times he did make it home.

One night, my brothers and I heard him kick at the front door until
it gave way.

Huddled beneath the galaxy of our Star Wars bedspread,
we listened to the floorboards as they whispered: living room,
hallway, kitchen.

Mike, the oldest, said: *We just need to make it through the night.*

Dad's voice burned through the dusty heating vents in the floor.

Ed, the middle brother, asked: *Where's the light saber?*

It's what we called our aluminum flashlight.
On camping trips, we'd slice through campfire smoke late into the evening.

Something hit the kitchen floor.
Then the sound of it being ripped apart; a slow splatter of liquid, dripping.

Ed gasped, *Oh my god, he got Mom!*

No, Mike shook his head. *It's the turkey.*
She was defrosting it earlier, remember?
Still, we shut our eyes to the sound of that cavernous mouth at work.

Ed grabbed my arm, *Whatever you do, don't go in the cellar.*

We didn't have a cellar.

Look, Mike said, *Somebody's got to go for help.*

Then a creak outside the door.

I could see the silhouette of Mike's mouth open, then close.

A slur of curses crashed against the door:
first a foot,
then a fist,
followed by his entire mass thudding against the walls.

I wanted to reach for the clown-covered faceplate of our light-switch
but none of us could move as our world cracked like the surface
of the bathroom mirror where he used to study his anger.

I'd like to say the door held,
but we couldn't afford a house that would keep a family safe from itself.

But the exertion, or the one part of the cheap wooden door that held
as the rest of it collapsed, something crumpled our father's body to the floor,
just inside our room.

We stared at him lying there until our silence grew shadows.

Then Mike tore the stillness with his whisper,
Ed, go get the flashlight.

Steve, you get the matches.

You're Undead Like The Cranberries, in My Head Like a Legend
by David Ohlsen

As you die
for what I know
will only be
the first time today
I don't try to warn you

I go back and forth
from your gray, green eyes
desperate as oysters
clapping for their robbed pearl
to your legs
kicking and dripping

I put my hand on
your warm, struggling belly
and try to talk to you
about the night we crashed into a circus tent
and had lion tamers calling us fuckheads
and you smirked a little
when you said your last words
"God damn you for trying to
make me laugh right now,
babe"

I didn't tell you
this virus, it'll turn ya
make you wanna spread it
you're gonna really be the bad girl
just like you've always wanted
no more people telling you
you're all bark
& no bite

Which is why I'm standing here
as you rise and groan
locked and loaded

This isn't Voodoo magic anymore

Bang

No palmed puffer fish powder
You're not gonna wake up
with a new lesson in your head
You're lost to yourself
and you're hungry

Bang

There's only you
and your puppet strings of razor wire
Only me
and my Remington 870 shotgun

Bang

You fall into a pale heap
Your face finally goes limp
yielding its contortions
and you look just like you would
when you were sleeping—

left cheek pressed to your left bicep
like you were trying to spoon yourself
your closed eyes oncoming eclipses

lips like
curtain call.

ADOLESCENCE
by Savanah Moore-Kondo

I got your blood pumping.
I know I did.
The way it falls to the floor
is like a good porter. It's foaming
on the ground and when my lips
hit—a dyslexic mumble leaving them,
I see stars and matchbox cars. 'Cause your muscles
falling victim to my wisdom teeth remind me
of childhood and mom.
I can smell a good breakfast again,
my favorite, even though dad always fried
bacon and eggs
and they never tasted—never felt quite like
I know your occipital lobe is gonna.

Teeth of the Dead, or Why It's Hard to Brainstorm with Folks from Smyrna, Tennessee

by Derrick C. Brown

Gary Jr: So what you're saying is Gary tried to play dead,
and they still ate him? Those sick fucks.

Marshall Radin: Yep. Sat on him like a warm toilet seat and bit right
in.

Gary Jr: He was a great and forthright stepdad to us.
I wish I knew him better. Shit. I wish I could cry. I'm too pissed to
cry.

Darla: Bless his soul, GJ. He didn't have a chance. I bet he went fast.

Spooky Joe: I bet he didn't.

Marshall Radin: Look, enough speculator allegation.
We are all soldiers now, whether we like it or we don't like it.
We need ideas. And we need 'em stat. This world's getting creepier
than a foam party in a small room.

Stevie: Well, what if we sneak up, hit them with clubs and bats?
Wham, Bam, Thank you, you're dead.

Spooky Joe: Nope. Gotta do the face. Shatter and splatter.
Marshall, say you must obliterate the face. Danny tried to
whack off their head with a reinforced mop
and their mouths were still chomping away, all cottonmouth-like.

Little Benny: 'Tis true.

Mr. Jenkins: Can we just remove their teeth?

Gary Jr: How we gonna do that? Pliers. Shit.

Mr. Jenkins: I suggest we bait them with candy and soda. Lace it with flesh.
Soon they will rot.
They can't eat our brains if they don't have teeth.

Darla: Yeah, but they could gum our brains, which to me is worse.

Marshall Radin: Someone tell Darla to not chime in. These are evil things that have prospered against us.
They don't have toothaches, or blood, or nerves.
I reckon their God-given grinders would grow back, like a lizard from hell.

Mr Jenkins: Them being from hell is heresay.
If we can make them unable to tear into us, we win.

Spooky Joe: I know by the light of the silvery dog dish,
evil will find its way to tear on in, even if it has to
gum and gnaw and heave and suck.

Darla: Really, with the suck?

Little Benny: Could we make them eat something else?

Gary Jr: Like what? Soap. Shit.

Mr. Jenkins: Dr. Mike? Will you tell them what you told me?

Dr. Mike Candledish: Sure. We caught one last summer. At the vet.
Watched it through the glass.
Tore into a cat's brain. It may not be the human brains themselves they need,
but the things that live within most brains.
All that miracle electricity,
the memory maker, the joy releaser, the heart rate controller,
the vision collector, the dream distiller. It might juice 'em up.

Stevie: He's right, Marhsall Radin. I have watched them feed in the parking lot from the roof of the T.G.I.Fridays. They were moaning and watching the birds.

Gary Jr: What did you see, Stevie?

Stevie: They was all maggoty molars and moaning tongues.
One bit in to the TGIF vice manager and it was an explosion
of goopdy goop...then an employee, flair all blood soaked
and flying everywhere. They ate the got damned flair!
Then onto the head and the meat in it.

Dr. Mike Candledish: That's substantia nigra.

Stevie: Thanks Dr. Mike. I could see it all.
The brain was colorful.
It was wild black mess,
the red of the blood vessels,
the white matter of nerves,
the gray noodles, meaty.

Dr. Mike Candledish: Actually about the three pounds of
multicolored matter.

Stevie: Yep and they was unloading it in their mouths
and fumbling the chunkies out their cavities and rotten holes.
Then, the weirdest thing, they were watching the birds.

Darla: I was up there too, sheriff. All them evil faces settling for a moment,
satisfied.
Once they was done with that manager's big head,
they seemed sad from being satisfied. Then they snapped out of it
and were watching the birds.

Little Benny: Are you sure they weren't just looking up?

Darla: Maybe, but they were either looking at the birds
or they were looking at the sky. Reaching up to it.

Spooky Joe: Sounds creeeeepy.

Marshall Radin: Okay. I know what we do.
Tonight, we meet me at the downtown aquarium.
A whale's brain is big ass.

Dr. Mike Candledish: Seventeen pounds.

Marshall Radin: Yep. If they want any brain,
we may have a way to distract them and beat them to death. In the face.
If they eat any fishy brain, we will show them the sea, and watch if
they can swim.

It should give us enough time to
find high ground,
stare at the unlit skyline,
and finally get some shut eye.

If they were watching birds, we could be in luck.
If they were just watching the sky, things could be bad.
They might have been getting orders.

Spooky Joe: The orders come from below.

Gary Jr: Shit. Fuck them and their demon dicks. Shit.
We're winning as long as we don't quit.
Who here feels alive!

Spooky Joe: I do.

EATING OUR WORDS
by Cole "Inky" Sarar

We never believed in them.
They were childhood campfire tales,
smoke and shadow,
the shuffle of an animal in the underbrush.

 Vampires hungered for
blood, red and wet, hot and vital, to their cold pallor.
They had no life; they symbolized a frozen heart.
Vampires lacked heart, compassion.
We were afraid of vampires.

Werewolves howled and ripped things apart—
furred over and full of animal frenzy,
they were all growls and snarling; they symbolized the wilderness.
Werewolves lacked humanity, language.
We were afraid of werewolves.

Zombies hungered for brains—
an empty carcass, speaking and yet not understanding a damn thing.
They shambled slow and senseless, unresponsive.
They symbolized a lack of intelligence.
We were not afraid of zombies.

Zombies, you can outrun.
They don't flip a cape and turn into a bat.
They don't have some sort of carnivore instinct,
chasing you with claws and fangs.
They have rigor mortis and one word repeated ad nauseum.

Brains.

And yeah, the dead rising from their graves sounds creepy,
but when they push free of the earth with a speed that rivals
spring carrots?
I have enough time to go to the garage and back for an axe.
Do you tremble at a creature less successful than a Facebook protest?
What do we want?

Brains!
When do we want them?
Brains!

Vampires and werewolves are that which we fear others becoming.
Zombies are just what we fear to become.
Slow and with just one goal, with no understanding of what they are,
like suit-and-tie cubicle ants, groaning
Brains.
Television watchers and pop-culture junkies
desiring only what exists in other peoples' heads.
Brains.

What did we have to fear?

Until it happened.
And like the difference between the holiday burning log channel
and your house's smoking ashes,
and you understand that this is beyond the horror of flashlights.

A combination of hungers and manias,
a young man thrown out of the Walker library multiple times
finally locked into the psychiatric ward for pica,
the bloodstains on the carpets in the stacks
where he'd destroyed an entire shelf of books
before security threw him out like a weed that keeps growing back,
they found one of his teeth underneath a metal shelving unit,
already lacerated with metal and glass.

They found hundreds of young men and women
electrocuted in their bedrooms and at their desks,
where the hunger had just grown too twisted.

Security was posted around Borders and Barnes & Noble,
cement barriers outside the central library,
which was closed until further notice.
Stakes around the garden, but the infestation was now unstoppable.
They suggested the cause was drugs, hypnotism, neurological disease.
Teens were separated from their cell phones,
for fear they might choke on them.

We'd read Fahrenheit 451. We didn't burn the books.
Well, most of us didn't.
We packed them up in attics and closets,
locked them in garages,
took the guns out of the glass cabinets and filled them with tomes.
We locked up the computers, the board games, the CDs, the DVDs.
But yes, there were bonfires.
And we locked ourselves into our dark houses and drew closed the blinds.

The mutation began in small towns in the Bible Belt,
with no books to read,
whatever virus or mania made humans hunger for knowledge
started whispering in lovers eyes,
they say a young woman was dragged off her boyfriend's body,
screaming "I gotta KNOW him. I gotta KNOW him!"
blood and gray matter tumbling off her tongue—PCP, they said.
It was the same day we found Matt in the attic room,
he'd unlocked the padlock and gone for his laptop.
The lacerations in his mouth, the teethmarks in the cracked screen.

We thought maybe the Amish would be resistant,
maybe rednecks or the Taliban or Republicans,
but this fever ran runners under every white picket fence,
across every ocean.
We were human.
We were Eve in the garden.
We needed to know.

Finally, those of us with the willpower or genetic resistance
left the cities, and found ourselves once again,
crowded around campfires,
shuddering at the sounds of animals in the underbrush,
singing the scarecrow's song to threaten each other.

I would not be just a nothin',
my head all full of stuffin,
my heart all full of pain.
I would dance and be merry,
life would be a ding-a-derry.
If I only had a brain…

13 Ways of Looking at a Baby (and Please Note: This Poem Has Nothing to Do with Zombies)

by Matt Mason

I
On the night
when it commences,
you have no way of weighing
how much
your life
will be altered.

II
When you come upon her
as she finishes devouring,
her dinner sprayed across her face,
down her arms, in the tangles
of her hair, she will stare.
Open her mouth.
Gasp out,
"Gaaaaaaaaaaaaa!"

III
She seems so slow down there.
You let your mind wander
just a squinch,
look back and, oh God:
danger!

IV
You only think she is down.
You feel like you've endured
a bone-jarring labor of Hercules but,
finally,
her eyes are closed,
finally
still.

Don't turn your back, watch her, the moment you turn away that cry
    will make your hair rise
again, you will have to scramble back, find a way to put her down
again,
never be sure
when it all
may be finally
done.

V
It
is absolutely amazing
what she
will put
in her mouth.

VI
She smiles
and the teeth
in her head
look like what's left
of a picket fence between the weeds
and the old dirt road.

VII
The dog
is always
the first
to get it.

VIII
They always give you some scientific explanation
of how this all came about.
Yet, still,
you have to keep asking:
How did this happen?
What has brought this
here?

IX
The way she will look at you
sometimes,
as if she does not know whether you are air
or flesh,
her eyes wide and wild,
sparkle of saliva quivering on her chin
as she lurches
for you.

X
For as long as
you might live,
they
are yours
and you
belong
to them.

XI
She is so
very small,
it can startle you
how strong she really is.

XII
You will imagine her face, sometimes,
as if it can tell you the truth
about whether God exists or not, about what
sort of universe
we inhabit.

XIII
Ask the father or mother
stumbling through the house in the darkest of the night,
pants God knows where:
they will tell you she has come
to eat
your
brains.

ZOMBIES' APOCALYPSE
by Jesse Parent

The flies.
They came in swarms.
In our single-mindedness,
we paid them no attention.
Sifting through their masses

I do not know what we were thinking,
if anything, at all.
Perhaps that the succulent flesh of the living
we devoured in our frenzied feeding
was their ultimate goal, as well.
They attached themselves
to our decaying skin
like remoras.
Our thrumming slow speech
combining with the buzzing of their wings
to sound a low note
like war horns,
driving the living before us.
Their screams of terror seasoning their delicious
BRAINS
like cinnamon.

The shadowed memories from our lives,
now former,
should have glistened a spark
of recognition of their true goal.

Karen was the first to notice,
her dangling eye swung on top of her broken skull.
Peripherally, her glassy orb detected the writhing inside.
Larvae wandering slowly through her cranial cavity,
wreaking havoc and destruction in their wake.
They were feasting on her
BRAINS.

The irony was not lost on us.

Karen called to me,
"Uhhrrrr. . . ."
"Karen!"
I replied.
"It sounds like you're having a stroke!"
"Uhhrrr. . . ."
She repeated,
before the ball joint of her jaw fell away,
her rotted tendons devoured,
the marauding maggots erupting from her one good eye.

Phillip screamed in horror,
dropping both halves of a warm kitten
he had found under the Vanderbilt's veranda.
"Karen, no!" he cried,
pointing with his graying right index finger.
Phillip's own veins writhed with pupae,
bursting forth, severing the hand at mid-forearm.
Newly formed nymphs
taking flight from hollowed arteries.
The buzzing of their wings combining with our thrumming moans
    of terror,
to sound a low note
like war horns.

The irony was not lost on us.

Our race hardly lasted a month.
Reduced from power incarnate to mere carrion.

Except for us lucky few
hidden in this freezer.
Phillip still stares wistfully at his absent arm,
murmuring Karen's name;
the parasites, dormant,
our own movement, slowed.

The sound of the living returning outside of these metal walls,
they keep us chilled, immobile, dormant.
Fearing the warmth that could return to our limbs and let loose our hunger.

I wonder if the irony is lost on them.

Tanka: Yet Another Poem About the Zombie Apocalypse Part 2
by Curtis X Meyer

The worst part about
the zombie apocalypse
won't be the smell, nor
wondering if we'll live, but
pretending it's not awesome.

Your Average Apocalypse
by Karen Garrabrant

it's already happened
and you know it
as you drape yourself
on a couch after a long day

it's in the bright, primary colors
of glossy commercials
you flip through
it's in the cars and burgers
insurance and pills
mega store and mega store
there's nothing quite as depressing
—and it is in the depression—
as night after night of television
urges you to rest

you watch crime scene dramas
smart pretty girls picking through gross things
swamps and guts
and then
your dreams wear lab coats and gloves

and you know it
as you drive to work every morning
and curse at lights
beneath overcast gray skies

under the signs, spinning
before a generation confused
by microfiche and card catalogues
you remember
that there was a thing called a record
grooved
a document of an event
books long ago forgotten
with ticker tape warnings inside

they are a muscle memory
a phantom appendage
and your tongue turns vinyl

you feel yourself slipping
crow's feet taloning your eyes
an uneasy sludge in your system
slowing you

they want your brains

they already have them

viral
like the ever present touch screens
the erasure of before moments gone digital
they are ubiquitous
and blameless
unknowable
remote

in suits and behind microphones
with sinister winks made behind clear frames
in sports uniforms
and monochromatic suits
they smile at you
pixilated
and gnawing

the pit in your gut grows
you stir honey with a spoon
make circles and calm yourself
with the sound of metal
on the edge of the mug
to alleviate the anxiety attack
with something that sounds old—ancient

but you know
you've read blurs of articles
and seen the moving maps of earth fevers
the hysterical reporters

the mockable warnings of forever-in-panic
infinite orange alert
the color of prisoner jumpsuits and cones on the highway
—no coincidence

you know there's a tidal churn of plastic bags
just like the cupboard you have overstuffed with them
and you feel the swirl of vomit
in your throat as oil spill after oil spill
engulfs
the oceans

we have all the answers
it doesn't have to be this way

but it will
because the world
has long since crossed apocalypse

it's just that
nobody can signify a date or a year
the expiration moved like gas
and now mama earth is taking it back

it's evident in the rule of zombies
overpopulating
seemingly immune to darwinism
and not to fanaticism
as old as their medieval lineage

and you know this

ATHANASIOS
by Baruch Porras-Hernandez

On this island
we assured ourselves
we would be safe, in paradise.
We ate
while people in the mainlands were devoured.
Listened to music, not really listening, just wondering,
when the television and radio went offline, we watched DVDs,
there is nothing do
but fuck and forget.
We expected refugees, prepared our rifles to protect our shelter and our food,
lit our joints with bills; money is now worthless.
 No one came.
The sea stayed blue and green,
and we held hands, walked on the beach.
She asked me one night, "Maybe we should have done something? To help?"
We fuck against the window; I like to watch the sea as I fuck her.
Last two humans on earth, I keep thinking, when the heads protrude
one by one, ten, fifteen, fifty, one hundred, then an army
all from the sea. They come. Wet, deformed, undead, and hungry.
I keep fucking her, put her hair in my mouth, try to make the last time matter,
don't tell her, that they've walked across an ocean
to eat us alive.

Performance Art in the Time of the Zombie
by David Macpherson

Grant money is no longer available
for artists to finance their work
(what with no governments or set monetary systems,
and the general threat of being bitten
by members of your audience),
but that does not stop several artists
from creating pieces that speak to their world.

An old school performance artist
stated, "This isn't different from Before.
Doing this kind of work is never wanted,
but that does not mean it's unnecessary."
She captures zombies and dresses them up
in themed costumes and then sends them
back into the infected zones.
Her piece "Send in the Clowns," where
she dressed 300 zombies to
look like Bozo the Clown, is still discussed.
She reports children across the safe zones
wake up screaming from dreams of ravenous Bozos.
The artist considers this a successful result.

Another artist makes a show
of eating the flesh of zombies
in his piece, "Turnabout Cuisine."
He butchers and prepares the flesh
of neutralized zombies in traditional
Japanese shabu shabu style,
dipping a thinly sliced sliver of Zombie
into a bowl of boiling water
long enough to burn away contagion
and make it delicious.
In lieu of an exhibition catalog,
he offers a zombie cookbook for sale.

In the past two years, he has sold twelve copies.
"It's becoming a movement," he says,
"it's the next new thing."

One art collective, the Undead Deschamps,
put on a show called "sneak attack,"
where in the middle of the night,
they dressed themselves as zombies
and pretended to attack zone citizens.
As with some art pieces,
they did not get the expected results.
It goes without saying, this
piece was performed only once.
The survivors of the collective
recall the performance warmly.

The artist who created the zombie piñata piece
has been embraced by several safe zones,
with offers inviting her to present the piece elsewhere.
She has declined the chance to continue with the work,
saying, "It's a hard piece to perform.
First you have to capture a zombie,
then you need to open up its belly,
fill it with candy, and sew it back.
I take pride in my needle work,
it's one of the important aspects of the piece,
so I don't skimp there.
Then I need helpers to truss it up
and hoist it over the compound.
The general public really loves this work.
You can see the joy on their faces
when the candy is released.
But there is more to me
than this one performance.
I'm not just the lady who beats
the candy-filled zombie with a stick.
I am so much more.
I am only just beginning my artistic journey."

One artist performed a piece entitled
"Transformation-Infestation,"
in which he let a zombie bite him.
He then sat in a lotus position as he
calmly waited for the typical metamorphosis.
The crowd was surprisingly thick
as they watched the slow change occur.
When the artist was burned away
and all that remained was the zombie,
the Zone Leader went over and cut off its head.
The artist had prepped the Zone Leader
in advance to say, "I don't know art,
but I know what I like," when he cut down.
For some reason, he didn't say that.
He trailed off, as if distracted.
He said, "I don't know. I just don't know."

LOVER
by Nick Spears

Screaming. Her lime green nails upon my face. "Pistachio," she called them. She hated when I called them "lime." She always loved those quirky colored nails. I, on the other hand, always loved her bright blue eyes. They always knew when I was lying. It's a funny thing how the thing I loved most about her, was the same thing that could see the evil in me. They taste terrible. Like a golf ball made of oyster, then dipped in olive juice. Maybe I'll try those fingers next?

Two Ways of Looking at the Zombie Apocalypse

by Victor Infante

1. Any 19 Lines Spoken by a Zombie Comprise a Villanelle (A Found Poem)

Brains. Braaaains. Braaaainnnns. Brains.
Brains. Brains. Braaaains.
Braaaainnnns. Brains. Braaaains. Braaaains.

Brains. Braaaains. Braaaainnnns. Brains.
Brains. Brains. Braaaains.
Brains. Braaaains. Braaaainnnns. Brains.

Braaaainnnns. Brains. Braaaains. Braaaains.
Brains. Brains. Braaaains.
Braaaainnnns. Brains. Braaaains. Braaaains.

Braaaainnnns. Brains. Braaaains. Braaaains.
Brains. Brains. Braaaains.
Brains. Braaaains. Braaaainnnns. Brains.

Braaaainnnns. Brains. Braaaains. Braaaains.
Brains. Brains. Braaaains.
Braaaainnnns. Brains. Braaaains. Braaaains.

Braaaainnnns. Brains. Braaaains. Braaaains.
Brains. Brains. Braaaains.
Brains. Braaaains. Braaaainnnns. Brains.
Braaaainnnns. Brains. Braaaains. Braaaains.

2. A Few Last Words from Mambo Before You Sleep

You cast a country as cathedral against dying,
pace behind locked doors, gates turned cages—
yet in your heart you knew that you were lying.

Life and death, Third World and First—
youth and wealth and unpaid wages.
You cast a country as cathedral against dying,

transformed religion into an unquenched thirst,
took lust and fear as map points, gauges.
Yet in your heart you knew that you were lying,

and that lie became a coiled snake, and worse,
transformed history to burning pages.
You cast a country as cathedral against dying,

and in the process swallowed deep a curse,
replacing God with empty faces,
yet in your heart you knew that you were lying:

from television, heroin and hearse,
to shambling, deathless night somnambulations—
you cast a country as cathedral against dying,
yet in your heart you knew that you were lying.

APOLOGIA OF THE UNDEAD
by Lindsay Miller

You think we do not run
because we can't. You think we are
too brokendown, too rottenthrough,
our muscles too gnawed for speed.
You see us leadarm lumbering
on sticky sidewalks and assume
that we, like you, are every second moving
as fast as we hungrily can.

You, with your ripe guts
churning savage, your hamstrings
that remember firelight tigerskulls,
you're the ones that count velocity.
It lives in the deep of your carnivore brainstems.
You think yourselves such hunters,
masters of physics and steel, you made
machines to outbeast the beasts,
but true predators don't need to chase.

Why should we? Decay
is on our side.

We walk because we are made to walk,
because we can, for the pleasure
of entropy crumbling our legs. We do not seek.
We are not hungry; we know
there will always be enough to eat.

You have so many enemies: gravity,
sharp edges, the skittering vermin
inside your blood. All we have to do
is wait until you spinesplinter
under the weight of your own skulls.
You are an eventual feast. Our jaws
are terribly patient.

THE LAST HIPSTER
by Brennan Bestwick

I liked that Cranberries song, "Zombie,"
long before the undead walked the streets
and those still living only played it ironically,
until it was back "in your heeeeeeaaaaad" again.
I still have a rare unopened 7" import
of the single collecting dust on my wall,
won in a late night eBay bidding war.
I'm over it.

Even with all the street shops savaged and looted,
I still wear whatever plaid flannel shirt
I find on the floor from the night before
spent spooning my shotgun. I will not sell out.
The zombies all look alike anywhere you see them,
ripped shirts with blood stained buttons and necks,
one long moaning, "uuuuuuuhhhhhhhhh-ing"
parade of cliché, a walking Gap ad for the un-alive.
It's not authentic or inspired.

Now, every tough guy that called me "queer" for wearing
scarves in summer is either no longer living or on the run,
envying the slingshot weapons of mass beheadings I managed
to MacGyver from these wool accessories worn
around my neck in any weather, purchased
from a long list of thrift stores few have ever heard of.
I load empty bottles of PBR like cannonballs,
launching them from my bedroom window
to burst against rotten flesh foreheads.

Weeks before the nightwalkers ate mailmen
and PTA mothers without picking up a fork,
I was the one eating everything raw and local.
I'm disciplined. I follow a vegan, low-cal,
all organic, gluten-free diet founded by a group
of defecting Tibetan monks I read about in a friend's zine.
My eating habits are ones of principle.

In all honesty, I don't find the zombies any worse than
most everyone else was, they're just as boring and predictable.
The only things I truly miss are the coffee shop downtown,
that Morrissey sweater my ex-girlfriend never returned,
and my cat, Sgt. Pepper.

I know my deadbolt won't last much longer,
but I have no plans of being devoured like the others.

It's too mainstream and pedestrian.

ADVENT
by Angus Adair

The wind howls
a list of terrorist demands.
I will not negotiate with the weather.
I make a bunker under the covers.
In the eye of the storm
I am king of my castle of quilts
with a crown made of paper.
My hands have powder burns
from Christmas crackers.
I live off what I can scavenge
from Advent calendars.
She dropped the bomb of breaking up
on December 23rd.
The shadows of romantic injuries past
grow longer
and lie like tripwires around the room.
The freezing rain wants in
like a relentless horde in a Romero movie.
I tell myself it`s going to be fine,
that she hasn't infected me
with a growing darkness
that I am not a simply running on muscle memory
that my heart has not become a zombie.
I tell myself it was only
a scratch.

Fuck A Nostradamus
by Jason Bayani

The final chapter of this world
will not arrive at the ass end of a big bang.
It will congeal, it will rail upon its own significance
It will grow a well-manicured beard and DJ dance parties
in gentrified neighborhoods
it will think itself
pregnant with thought and fine cheese, preface
even the most trivial of its actions
as being done "Apocalypse–style".
It will quote itself often, in Facebook status updates:
I am the greatest disaster of this generation of this decade— The Apocalypse
Why won't you let me be great?— The Apocalypse
The end is nigh— The Apocalypse

The Apocalypse will dedicate two hours out of its day to write
long-winded blog posts about how everyone else
is *such a fuckin' douchebag*. It will also claim
that it is not a hipster.

It will be heralded by the roving band of shirt cockers
who speak only in the silent languages of *hey, look at my dick,*
can you see my dick? I'm just wearing a shirt with no pants
to accentuate the fact that my dick is hanging out, no reason
I like a cool breeze. Hey, is that my dick? It sure is.

We will learn that creativity had never died
it was busy trying to figure out how many different ways
we could achieve an orgasm.
There will be much pillow-fucking.
There will be much volume.

The Apocalypse will come
and it will become very upset
when you are not comfortable in its presence
because it makes them uncomfortable
and the Apocalypse does not like to be uncomfortable

especially when you stigmatize it with such trigger words as
extinction level event and *organismist*;
Then the Apocalypse will get mad at all the people,
say that they're the ones who are being organisimists against it,
and when the people say,
perhaps you don't understand the power dynamics at work here,
also, you're not an organism,
the Apocalypse will storm off in a huff rambling about political correctness
and bootstraps; somehow it'll end up being all the dead people's fault
for not being the civil ones in this conversation.

And there will be those who join the fray
there will be those who will claim to be above it
and there will be those who will write it off
as just one big corporate/freemason/lizard person conspiracy.

And we left will be the worst of all;
amongst the death and building fracture
all anyone will know how to talk about
is how this much tragedy really makes living difficult on them.
How we will still clamor for attention from a diminishing audience.
Inevitably, there will be that asshole
who will loudly proclaim that humility and process
in the face of impending doom is "totally gay bro".
And when we greet each other, it will not be
with a smile or a handshake, but a simple disclaimer
It's the end of the world and we're all probably gonna die soon, wanna fuck?
It will be the bright spot of our humanity
our most precious act of giving
and the zombies, by this point
will simply lose their taste for us.

NEW WRITE BLOODY BOOKS FOR 2011

Dear Future Boyfriend
Cristin O'Keefe Aptowicz's debut collection of poetry tackles
love and heartbreak with no-nonsense honesty and wit.

38 Bar Blues
C. R. Avery's second book, loaded with bar-stool musicality and brass-knuckle poetry.

Workin' Mime to Five
Dick Richard is a fired cruise ship pantomimist. You too can learn
his secret, creative pantomime moves. Humor by Derrick Brown.

Reasons to Leave the Slaughter
Ben Clark's book of poetry revels in youthful discovery from the heartland
and the balance between beauty and brutality.

Birthday Girl with Possum
Brendan Constantine's second book of poetry examines the invisible lines
between wonder & disappointment, ecstasy & crime, savagery & innocence.

Yesterday Won't Goodbye
Boston gutter punk Brian Ellis releases his second book of poetry,
filled with unbridled energy and vitality.

Write About an Empty Birdcage
Debut collection of poetry from Elaina M. Ellis that flirts with loss,
reveres appetite, and unzips identity.

These Are the Breaks
Essays from one of hip-hops deftest public intellectuals, Idris Goodwin

Bring Down the Chandeliers
Tara Hardy, a working-class queer survivor of incest, turns sex,
trauma and forgiveness inside out in this collection of new poems.

1,000 Black Umbrellas
The first internationally released collection of poetry
by old school author Daniel McGinn.

The Feather Room
Anis Mojgani's second collection of poetry explores storytelling and
poetic form while traveling farther down the path of magic realism.

Love in a Time of Robot Apocalypse
Latino-American poet David Perez releases his first book
of incisive, arresting, and end-of-the-world-as-we-know-it poetry.

The New Clean
Jon Sands' poetry redefines what it means to laugh, cry, mop it up and start again.

Sunset at the Temple of Olives
Paul Suntup's unforgettable voice merges subversive surrealism
and vivid grief in this debut collection of poetry.

Gentleman Practice
Righteous Babe Records artist and 3-time International Poetry Champ
Buddy Wakefield spins a nonfiction tale of a relay race to the light.

How to Seduce a White Boy in Ten Easy Steps
Debut collection for feminist, biracial poet Laura Yes Yes
dazzles with its explorations into the politics and metaphysics of identity.

Hot Teen Slut
Cristin O'Keefe Aptowicz's second book recounts stories of
a virgin poet who spent a year writing for the porn business.

Working Class Represent
A young poet humorously balances an office job with the life
of a touring performance poet in Cristin O'Keefe Aptowicz's third book of poetry

Oh, Terrible Youth
Cristin O'Keefe Aptowicz's plump collection commiserates and celebrates
all the wonder, terror, banality and comedy that is the long journey to adulthood.

OTHER WRITE BLOODY BOOKS (2003 - 2010)

Great Balls of Flowers (2009)
Steve Abee's poetry is accessible, insightful, hilarious, compelling,
upsetting, and inspiring. TNB Book of the Year.

Everything Is Everything (2010)
The latest collection from poet Cristin O'Keefe Aptowicz,
filled with crack squirrels, fat presidents, and el Chupacabra.

Catacomb Confetti (2010)
Inspired by nameless Parisian skulls in the catacombs of France,
Catacomb Confetti assures Joshua Boyd's poetic immortality.

Born in the Year of the Butterfly Knife (2004)
The Derrick Brown poetry collection that birthed Write Bloody Publishing.
Sincere, twisted, and violently romantic.

I Love You Is Back (2006)
A poetry collection by Derrick Brown.
"One moment tender, funny, or romantic, the next, visceral, ironic,
and revelatory—Here is the full chaos of life." (Janet Fitch, *White Oleander*)

Scandalabra (2009)
Former paratrooper Derrick Brown releases a stunning collection of poems written
at sea and in Nashville, TN. About.com's book of the year for poetry

Don't Smell the Floss (2009)
Award-winning writer Matty Byloos' first book of bizarre, absurd, and deliciously
perverse short stories puts your drunk uncle to shame.

The Bones Below (2010)
National Slam Champion Sierra DeMulder performs and teaches
with the release of her first book of hard-hitting, haunting poetry.

The Constant Velocity of Trains (2008)
The brain's left and right hemispheres collide in Lea Deschenes' Pushcart-Nominated
book of poetry about physics, relationships, and life's balancing acts.

Heavy Lead Birdsong (2008)
Award-winning academic poet Ryler Dustin releases his most
definitive collection of surreal love poetry.

Uncontrolled Experiments in Freedom (2008)
Boston underground art scene fixture Brian Ellis
becomes one of America's foremost narrative poetry performers.

Ceremony for the Choking Ghost (2010)
Slam legend Karen Finneyfrock's second book of poems ventures
into the humor and madness that surrounds familial loss.

Pole Dancing to Gospel Hymns (2008)
Andrea Gibson, a queer, award-winning poet who tours with Ani DiFranco,
releases a book of haunting, bold, nothing-but-the-truth ma'am poetry.

City of Insomnia (2008)
Victor D. Infante's noir-like exploration of unsentimental truth and poetic exorcism.

The Last Time as We Are (2009)
A new collection of poems from Taylor Mali, the author
of "What Teachers Make," the most forwarded poem in the world.

In Search of Midnight: the Mike Mcgee Handbook of Awesome (2009)
Slam's geek champion/class clown Mike McGee on his search for midnight
through hilarious prose, poetry, anecdotes, and how-to lists.

Over the Anvil We Stretch (2008)
2-time poetry slam champ Anis Mojgani's first collection: a Pushcart-Nominated
batch of backwood poetics, Southern myth, and rich imagery.

Animal Ballistics (2009)
Trading addiction and grief for empowerment and humor with her poetry,
Sarah Morgan does it best.

Rise of the Trust Fall (2010)
Award-winning feminist poet Mindy Nettifee
releases her second book of funny, daring, gorgeous, accessible poems.

No More Poems About the Moon (2008)
A pixilated, poetic and joyful view of a hyper-sexualized,
wholeheartedly confused, weird, and wild America with Michael Roberts.

Miles of Hallelujah (2010)
Slam poet/pop-culture enthusiast Rob "Ratpack Slim" Sturma
shows first collection of quirky, fantastic, romantic poetry.

Spiking the Sucker Punch (2009)
Nerd heartthrob, award-winning artist and performance poet,
Robbie Q. Telfer stabs your sensitive parts with his wit-dagger.

Racing Hummingbirds (2010)
Poet/performer Jeanann Verlee releases an award-winning book
of expertly crafted, startlingly honest, skin-kicking poems.

Live for a Living (2007)
Acclaimed performance poet Buddy Wakefield releases his second collection
about healing and charging into life face first.

WRITE BLOODY ANTHOLOGIES

The Elephant Engine High Dive Revival (2009)
Our largest tour anthology ever! Features unpublished work by
Buddy Wakefield, Derrick Brown, Anis Mojgani and Shira Erlichman!

The Good Things About America (2009)
American poets team up with illustrators to recognize the beauty and wonder in our
nation. Various authors. Edited by Kevin Staniec and Derrick Brown

Junkyard Ghost Revival (2008)
Tour anthology of poets, teaming up for a journey of the US in a small van.
Heart-charging, socially active verse.

The Last American Valentine:
Illustrated Poems To Seduce And Destroy (2008)
Acclaimed authors including Jack Hirschman, Beau Sia, Jeffrey McDaniel,
Michael McClure, Mindy Nettifee and more. 24 authors and 12 illustrators
team up for a collection of non-sappy love poetry. Edited by Derrick Brown

Learn Then Burn (2010)
Exciting classroom-ready anthology for introducing new writers
to the powerful world of poetry. Edited by Tim Stafford and Derrick Brown.

Learn Then Burn Teacher's Manual (2010)
Turn key classroom-safe guide Tim Stafford and Molly Meacham
to accompany *Learn Then Burn*: A modern poetry anthology for the classroom.

Knocking at the Door: Poems for Approaching the Other (2011)
An exciting compilation of diverse authors that explores the concept of the Other
from all angles. Innovative writing from emerging and established poets.

WWW.WRITEBLOODY.COM